books designed with giving in mind

Crepes & Omelets
Microwave Cooking
Vegetable Cookbook
Kid's Arts and Crafts
Bread Baking
The Crockery Pot Cookbook
Kid's Garden Book
Classic Greek Cooking
The Compleat American
    Housewife 1776
Low Carbohydrate Cookbook

Kid's Cookbook
Italian
Cheese Guide & Cookbook
Miller's German
Quiche & Souffle
To My Daughter, With Love
Natural Foods
Chinese Vegetarian
Jewish Gourmet
Working Couples

Mexican
Sunday Breakfast
Fisherman's Wharf Cookbook
Ice Cream Cookbook
Hippo Hamburger
Blender Cookbook
The Wok, a Chinese Cookbook
Cast Iron Cookbook
Japanese Country
Fondue Cookbook

from nitty gritty productions

HIPPO COOK BOOK

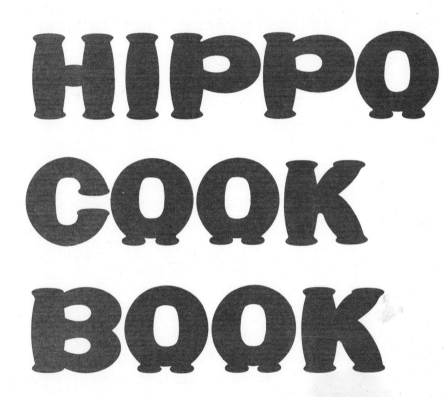

text by
Jack Falvey

Illustrations
by "Wolo"

A Nitty Gritty Book*
Published by
Nitty Gritty Productions
P. O. Box 5457
Concord, California 94524

*Nitty Gritty Books - Trademark
Owned by Nitty Gritty Productions
Concord, California

ISBN 0-911954-08-2

For my wife Pat
and my son Tim

Jack Falvey

To Lydia my wife,
to Lotte my sister, and
to my friends "Skip" and "Jackie" Matthews
who love good food,
and to all the good HIPPOPOTAMUSSERS in
the blue Nile!

"Wolo"

TABLE OF CONTENTS

INTRODUCTION

The original Hippo at Van Ness Avenue and Pacific in San Francisco was once a large, barren building occupied by a Safeway store. With some paint, imagination, and Wolo, an airy attractive restaurant was created. The cooking area was set in the center of the room, and crowned with a huge hopper hood. Because the building was large and our hamburgers were to be the same, I named the restaurant The Hippopotamus.

I will never forget Wolo's first visit to that huge empty store . . . It was on a Sunday morn. Wolo took one look at the top of the 18 foot ceiling, panicked and gasped, "I have never drawn anything so large!" He looked down to the floor strewn with debris and found a 6 foot long stick—he tied a piece of chalk on the end of it—mounted a ladder and balancing the long stick started to draw a circle . . . I left for church! . . . When I returned an hour later this genius had created my logo. The Hippo that is on the cover of this book!

My first hamburger was big but it wasn't terribly unusual—except that it was charcoal broiled. After observing customers eating hamburgers for dinner night after night, it became apparent that there was indeed a demand for variety in this specialized field. Little by little, I added more kinds of hamburgers to the menu. First, the Chiliburger—our own chili was spooned over the top of the hamburger and garnished with chopped onions. My next creation was the Frenchburger—I took our glorious Danish Bleu Cheese salad dressing, poured it over our hamburger, crossed it with crisp bacon strips and quartered the top of the roll. I placed the quarters symmetrically around the patty—ate it with a knife and fork—and used the top quarters for dunking—*Terrific*! I soon developed other ideas, many from my visits to restaurants in foreign countries and I created new sauces—to compliment the American hamburger. We now have 57 varieties of the hamburger and the hamburger steak!

You can dress up a hamburger in many ways—you can give it sauce—you can give it eye appeal, but you must remember: The meat that makes up the hamburger makes it a success! When I buy hamburger I go to my favorite butcher shop and pick out the cut or cuts I want. Top round is best—chuck is next. But for economy, you can select other cuts—mix them together—but never use any so-called "innards" . . . just the flesh meat and always Grade A. I always ask my butcher to trim the meats of heavy tendons and then have it put through the grinder twice. This process assures good mixing of the fat and grinding of any small tendons missed by trimming. I add suet when necessary to bring the total fat content to 7% for pan frying and about 15% for gas/electric or charcoal broiling. Ground meat, when cooked without suet, is very dry.

One thing you must remember; use freshly ground hamburger. The sooner you cook your meat after grinding, the better! If you expect a great hamburger, for heaven's sake, don't freeze the ground meat.

Forming your ground meat correctly into a patty I consider very important. The less you touch the patty—the greater the finished product. One of my largest problems in the operation of The Hippo restaurants is the cooks who insist on over-*patting* the meat patties. As you know, nothing will do more to toughen the meat.

In order to create a perfect hamburger patty or steak, I form them with great care. I always handle the meat as if it were a fresh egg—passing it gently from one hand to the other, forming it into a ball. I now place it on a table, and, with as few light touches as possible, pat to the desired thickness. A thick patty is best—the thinner the patty the drier the finished product. One-third of a pound, about 1 1/4" to 1 1/2" thick, is the perfect size. Larger hamburgers for the big guys can run to 1/2 pound! If you are making hamburger steaks, 1/2 pound should be the weight and *this* patty should be oval-shaped to give it the eye appeal of a New York cut.

One legend maintains that the original hamburger was named after the city of Hamburg in Germany. The story goes that around 1700, when the sailors from that city came to New York, they showed the local wharf cooks how to chop up meat, shape it into patties and cook it. So the early New Yorkers called it "hamburger." However, it wasn't until after the St. Louis Fair in 1903, to be exact, that the real popularity of the hamburger began. It seems that a restaurant started selling a crudely shaped patty—cooked on a griddle—sandwiched between two slices of bread. It was the hit of the St. Louis Fair and developed from a fad into an American tradition.

Certainly a week does not go by in an American home today that hamburger is not used in some form or another. If it is not in the form of a patty or a steak—it appears in a meat loaf, a sauce, a dolmas, or a casserole. In fact, I am sure the hamburger has become the most popular meat dish in this country since good *ole' Louis* took her to the fair!

In the cooking of the hamburger patty, there is one school that maintains a charcoal cooked patty is the best . . . others prefer to avoid the charcoal, which does tend to give the patty a smokey, and therefore, heavier taste. Some prefer to broil the meat—and others love it cooked in an iron skillet with a dry, salted pan bottom—or in melted butter!

When I charcoal broil a hamburger patty, I cook it on one side without turning till the red juices bubble on top. DO NOT keep turning—a revolving hamburger is a dry hamburger. Then, I turn it over for an equal amount of time and presto—there is a beautifully cooked rare hamburger! If the meat is cooked correctly—RARE—it is *firm* to the touch.

If one of my guests *must* have a well done hamburger, I simply cook it longer on each side. Under no circumstances do I ever press the patty with a spatula, this will simply turn the texture of the meat to sawdust.

Then there is the other extreme of preparing hamburger . . . steak tartare . . . We call it the Cannibalburger—RAW—uncooked—extremely appealing to a small number of humans. It's secret besides its condiments, is FRESH ground meat—the better the quality—the better! No suet please—and be sure to serve it well chilled. For fluffs and condiments for the steak tartare see page 104.

In my recipes in this book which are adapted to the hamburger, are some short cuts and some economy cuts. If you are trying to economize, for heaven's sake DON'T do it on the *quality* of the ingredients in your cooking.

If the recipe calls for onions—be sure you get the freshest onions you can find . . . If it says Worcestershire sauce, use the best brand. We have made it a rule at The Hippo to always use the finest ingredients and condiments. Do yourself a favor and do the same in *your* home!

I always delay making my hamburger patties till it is close to cooking time. I always keep the ground meat COLD till cooking time. Patties that are made in advance dry out!

I NEVER PUT ANYTHING IN MY GROUND MEAT . . . I POUR MY SAUCES OVER THE TOP!

1/4 cup onions, chopped fine
1 pinch granulated garlic
1/4 lb. hamburger
3 1/3 teaspoons imported Mexican paprika
2 Tablespoons chile powder
1 pinch Cayenne pepper
1/4 cup tomato puree
1/2 cup hot water
1 pinch salt

THE CHILIBURGER (CHILE BEANS)

My mother used to make these beans with the very same recipe but she used kidney beans. Either way—it will be hard to find a better dish of chili frijoles!

In your earthenware pot put 1/2 lb. red pinto beans, 1 teaspoon salt and a tablespoon of minced onions. Soak them overnight. The beans will now have swollen and absorbed most of the water. Be sure beans are covered with water—place over low flame—cook till tender (approximately 1 hour), continuing to add water to cover the beans while cooking. Do not drain, let cool and liquid will turn to a solid.

While the beans are simmering away, start in on the second phase. Have the ingredients listed on the opposite page ready. Now saute the onions till transparent. Add garlic. Now add the hamburger and fork the meat into small pieces—when meat turns gray add the rest of the ingredients. Bring to a boil and then turn down and simmer for 15 minutes.

Add to the hot beans and simmer together for 1/2 hour. These chili beans can do nothing but get better in the next three days . . . the Mexican gentlemen will tell you "los frijoles con chile son mejores cuando están blanditos" (the longer you hold the beans the better they get).

THE CHEESEBURGER

The classic American cheeseburger has a slice of melted American cheese on top of the patty and we Americans love it! But, have you ever tried your next favorite cheese? Wow! What a treat . . . . . Swiss is great—Tybo is excellent—Teleme, beautiful—but my favorite is . . . . . BLEU CHEESE!* . . . . . Try any cheese you like—I have never had the courage—to try ripe limburger!

*Crumble 2 oz. of Bleu cheese and form it into a mini patty, and when you turn your patty over, put the Bleu cheese on top.

THE HIPPOBURGER
(OUR FAMOUS HUGE 1/2 LB. HAMBURGER)

I named this hamburger after the Hippopotamus. It is soooooo big it is positively vulgar . . . it is almost toooo much to eat. To eat this hamburger you must cast aside the table manners mother taught you and eat without benefit of fork or knife and the juices are not to be wasted . . . lick your fingers and dunk, and no one will accuse you of being in bad taste! On the contrary, the word "delicious" may have been invented for this giant, undelicate, regal, juicy 1/2 lb. Hippoburger covered with melted lush Martins New York Cheddar cheese.

10

OUR OWN BARBEQUE RELISH

Long ago we created a beautiful barbeque relish to eat with our plain hamburgers. The customers adore it—here is the recipe:

1/2 cup ketchup
1 cup tomato puree
1/2 cup sweet pickle relish
3/4 cup chopped onions
1 pinch ground pepper
1 pinch Cayenne pepper
1 pinch salt

Mix the above ingredients together . . . Serve it cold . . . Keep it refrigerated.

SESAME SEEDS

When I first opened The Hippo we had a jar of toasted sesame seeds on each table. The customers loved them sprinkled on top of the patty . . . . . Unfortunately, they loved them so much they would walk away with the seeds—jar and all! They are long since gone from the table—but our special rolls are topped with sesame seeds.

Have some of these seeds on hand at home—toast them and use them as a condiment with the hamburger!

THE ISLANDBURGER

On top of your hamburger patty place a round of pineapple—now cover with about 3 oz. of my Thousand Island dressing (see page 120). Put a red cherry in the hole . . . . . sprinkle with chopped parsley. Quarter the bun top and place symmetrically around the patty --- Great on a bright sunny day!

13

14

THE BERKELEY BURGER

I named this hamburger in honor of the University of California in Berkeley because it is an integration of wild spices, and at that time, believe me, U. C. was wild!

1/2 cup mayonnaise
2 teaspoons prepared mustard
2 teaspoons Lea & Perrins Worcestershire sauce
2 cups finely grated Cheddar cheese
1 - 4 oz. can pimentos
1/4 teaspoon Accent

Combine all ingredients in blender and blend till smooth. Heat in a double boiler and spoon over the bun-mounted patty. Succulent!

THE STANFORDBURGER (FOR FOUR HUNGRY *HE-MEN*)

At the center of the Stanford University Campus stands the Hoover Library Tower --- This great shaft rises from the flat valley of the campus, which was probably Hoover's last erection. Ron Jones tried to copy this *Freudian* edifice in our hamburger!

After you have shaped 4 - 1/3 lb. meat patties and prepared the other condiments, cook the patties—melt two slices of cheese on top of each patty and toast the buns. To put this concoction together, follow the diagram and you will have a gorgeous new hamburger version of the old submarine sandwich.

Now have ready the following and follow the diagram:

8 slices tomato   *4 cups shredded lettuce*
8 slices onion   *4 - 6" bamboo skewers*
8 slices bell pepper (rings)   *4 cherry tomatoes (or 4 olives)*

potato chips or french fries for four.

17

THE JOE'SBURGER

When it comes to the hamburger I am a purist . . . I do not put seasoning in when preparing my meat . . . not even salt or pepper. Now comes the one exception . . . this is the hamburger that was started at San Francisco's old Chutes At The Beach–*hot dog* stands. They chopped onions and mixed them *into* the meat. It was later picked up by Joe's restaurant in North Beach and we now call it the "Joe'sburger!" and garnish it with some peperoncini–a particularly great Italian pepper that so compliments this hamburger.

Some rules are made to be broken–in cooking, be sure you break the right rule!

JOE'S SPECIAL

There is hardly an Italian restaurant in *our* North Beach that does not claim to have invented this one—I believe it was Joe Vanessi of that famous restaurant of the same name.

This is another old San Francisco hamburger concoction . . . For four persons use:

1 1/2 lb. hamburger
3 Tablespoons chopped onions
1 package frozen chopped spinach
3 eggs

Preheat your iron skillet with 3 tablespoons olive oil. Break the meat up in the pan and keep it separated. Add the onions. Add the spinach (precooked according to the directions on the package). Keep working the ingredients with a longhandled fork. When meat appears quite done, fork in the three eggs right from the shell. Spatula it up onto plates --- Serve with a generous amount of ketchup. Buno Gusto!

21

SAUTÉED ONIONS

Sautéed onions certainly go great with hamburgers. Scoop them on top of a hamburger steak—and call it like we do at The Hippo—The San Franciscan. Here's how you do it . . .

Thinly slice a large round onion, and when you do, to prevent crying, do as my old gourmet friend Philip Block Rosenthal of old Romanoff's restaurant does—chew on two kitchen stick matches—sulphur end *out* . . . and believe it or not you will not cry! Now saute these onions, *not the matches,* in butter—with not too much butter as the onions have their own juices. When soft and nice and brownish—pick them up with tongs—holding and shaking above the pan to remove excess juice. Place on top of the steak—garnish with chopped parsley. If you're over 50, follow with Tums!

A GRASSBURGER (SOMETIMES KNOWN AS A POTBURGER)

Into the patty work your refined grass. Knead it in and enjoy the Laugh-In.

THE BOURBONBURGER (ONE OF OUR FIRST HAMBURGERS)

Marinate a patty in salt and peppered straight bourbon for one hour. Cook the patty, place on bun bottom, pour the marinade over the patty. Cut the toasted bun top in quarters and use to dunk. The reason this hamburger did not last long on our menu was that the cooks would drink the bourbon—salt, pepper and all!

25

THE FRENCH CONNECTION

SAUCE FOR 6 SERVINGS

1 1/2 Tablespoons butter
1/2 pound yellow onions sliced crosswise
1 Tablespoon Bovril (an excellent condensed beef broth)
salt and pepper to taste
1/2 teaspoon Lea & Perrins Worchestershire sauce
1/2 pint dry vermouth

In a big frying pan saute the onions with melted butter until the onions are translucent. Now add the other ingredients and keep stirring until the sauce simmers and ingredients are thoroughly mixed.

Serve on a HAMBURGER PATTY (preferably in an individual casserole). Cover with the sauce—scooping up generous amounts of onions. Serve with hunks of French bread to help mop up this glorious sauce.

THE MUSHROOM BURGER

It's just our best seller . . . made with fresh mushrooms* in a beautiful gravy** . . . fit for a king!

*You can tell a fresh mushroom if the underpart around the stem is closed tight as a virgin.
**To a pint of hot gravy (recipe on page 129) add 1 lb. of thinly sliced fresh mushrooms—bring to a simmer and serve over the hamburger.

GARLICBURGER

Take two conventional slices of toasted French bread and brush with melted garlic butter (Page 138)—wrap it around a 1/3 lb. rare hamburger patty—indulge yourself—it's later than you think.

Or, if you are really daring, take 30 kernels of shelled garlic . . . fry till brown in olive oil, arrange evenly on a slice of toasted French bread, place the patty on top, place another piece of toasted French bread on top of the patty . . . after eating—retire to a windmill!

29

WESTERNBURGER (WESTERN "BARBEQUE" SAUCE)

1 1/2 cup tomato puree
1/2 cup water
2 Tablespoons oil
2 Tablespoons Lea & Perrins Worcestershire sauce
1 Tablespoon red wine vinegar
1 Tablespoon DRY mustard
1 teaspoon chile powder
1 teaspoon brown sugar
1/4 teaspoon granulated garlic
1/2 Tablespoon smoked salt

Combine above ingredients and simmer for 10 minutes. Garnish with a thin slice of center cup of bell pepper. Barbeque your steaks or patties for this one—and serve from the saddle just like home on the range.

THE TACOBURGER

Being a purist—relative to the hamburger patty—I must protect this commitment by explaining that the Tacoburger is not a *patty* per se, but rather hamburger meat spiced and cooked, and we call it "Mexican Meat Mix" (see page 79).

To present this great Mexican morsel to your diners, I suggest you spoon a generous amount of this loose spiced ground meat over half   a toasted hamburger bun and garnish with tortilla chips . . . red pepper . . . and a miniature Mexican flag!

33

34

SI!

MEXICANBURGER

1 1/2 cups water
1 Tablespoon beef concentrate
1/2 cup tomato puree
1 1/2 Tablespoons chili powder
2 Tablespoons dry white wine

1 teaspoon Maggi seasoning
1 small pinch Cayenne pepper
1 pinch salt
1 pinch pepper
1/2 teaspoon Worcestershire sauce

Bring to a boil. Simmer for 1/2 hour. Thicken with flour and water to the consistency of cream. Ladle over your hamburger.

OLÉBURGER

The hamburger with Guacamole . . . I have described how to set this hamburger up and how to make Guacamole on page 105.

SPANISH SAUCE (PEASANT STYLE)

1 cup water
1 teaspoon beef concentrate
1/2 cup solid pack tomatoes
1/4 cup tomato puree
2 Tablespoons sliced green pimento-stuffed olives
1 Tablespoon chopped parsley
1/4 of a crushed garlic bud
1 bay leaf
1/2 cup onions, diced
1/4 cup green peppers, diced
2 Tablespoons celery stalk, diced
1/2 teaspoon Maggi seasoning
1/4 teaspoon Lea & Perrins Worcestershire sauce

1 pinch salt
1 pinch ground pepper
1 pinch Accent

Bring water, beef concentrate and tomatoes to a boil. Add the other ingredients and simmer together 1/2 hour. Spoon over your hamburger—olé!

37

38

THE PIZZABURGER

Now here is one of the easiest and most popular hamburgers to make.

Go to your favorite pizza parlor and buy a pint of their pizza sauce --- or from a grocery store get two 8 oz. cans of pizza sauce . . . to this add:

1/2 lb. sliced raw mushrooms
1 teaspoon oregano
1 Tablespoon finely chopped parsley
1 small kernel crushed garlic
1 teaspoon Lea & Perrins Worcestershire sauce

In your dutch oven with a tablespoon of olive oil, sauté onions till transparent. Now add all of the ingredients—stir—bring to a boil—reduce heat and simmer 5 minutes.* Spoon over burger.

*The difference between boiling and simmering is about two notches on your stove control handle. When it's *boiling* you get plenty of bubbles and you had better stir it or it will stick to the bottom of the pot and burn! To *simmer* is to observe a few bubbles in the liquid . . .

STROGANOFFBURGER

1 teaspoon butter, melted
3 oz. chopped onions
1 oz. thinly sliced fresh mushrooms
1/2 teaspoon beef base mixed with 1/2 teaspoon warm water
1 teaspoon Maggi
1 teaspoon Lea & Perrins Worcestershire sauce
salt and pepper to taste
1 pint (16 oz.) sour cream

Sauté the onions in butter over a low flame. **DO NOT** let them get brown. Add mushrooms and simmer for about 5 minutes --- stirring continually. Add the balance of the ingredients and stir in. Allow to cool off.

When just warm add the "room temperature" sour cream—stir in well. Now heat under a very low flame—stirring continually until warm and blended—**DO NOT** allow even to simmer or the sour cream will crack.

40

41

RUSSIANBURGER (RED CABBAGE)

I asked my friend Ryann L. San Filippo'Abeel to give me her recipe for this delicious spiced red cabbage—it is so good and especially when served over the hamburger. Spoon just a glob of sour cream on top for taste, texture and eye appeal.

3 Tablespoons bacon fat
1/2 cup onions, sliced and wedged
1/2 cup apples, chopped
2/3 can Campbell's beef bouillon
3 Tablespoons red wine
3 Tablespoons red wine vinegar
1/2 bay leaf

1 teaspoon salt
1/2 teaspoon pepper
1 teaspoon dill weed
1 teaspoon Accent
2 Juniper berries —cracked and crushed
1 quart loosely packed red cabbage

First heat the onions and bacon fat in a dutch oven for about 5 minutes (or until the onions are transparent.) Slowly add the balance of the ingredients in listed order stirring continually and simmer for one hour.

43

WELSHBURGER

You will never find a better hamburger or a better recipe for a Welsh Rarebit!

WELSH RAREBIT

3 Tablespoons butter
5 Tablespoons flour
1 1/2 teaspoons paprika
1 pint milk, warm
1 teaspoon Lea & Perrins Worcestershire Sauce

5 oz. New York cheddar cheese
1 1/2 teaspoons dry mustard
1 teaspoon salt
1/2 teaspoon coarse ground pepper
3/4 cup beer

Fancy that—a *Welsh* Rarebit made with *New York* cheddar, yet!

Mix butter and flour into a roux. Now add paprika and slowly add *warm* milk, stirring constantly. Add Worcestershire and cheddar cheese (I stir this with a French whip) and continue to stir over low heat until the cheese is melted. Now I add mustard, salt and pepper. The consistency should now be rather thick so we add the beer . . . for flavor and to thin your sauce.

THE GAMEBURGER

This is a remarkable old English game sauce . . . my grandfather brought from Ireland. My father used to fill the cavity of a wild duck with it—sew it up—and after roasting the duck pour the same sauce over his wild rice — Magnificent! If you are ever lucky enough to get some wild duck—no less the wild rice—don't forget this sauce! In the meantime it goes remarkably well with charcoal broiled hamburgers.

1 cup currant jelly
2 Tablespoons bacon fat
4 Tablespoons water
1 garlic kernel, squashed
1/2 teaspoon lemon juice
5 teaspoons Lea & Perrins Worcestershire sauce
1/4 cup sherry wine

1/4 cup bourbon
1 Tablespoon ketchup
1/2 teaspoon paprika
1/4 teaspoon salt

Melt down the jelly with the water and bacon fat. Add the balance of the ingredients and simmer for 10 minutes.

48

LONDONBURGER

Equal parts sour cream and horseradish --- Electric! If you like your hamburger electrified!

When you ladle this over the hamburger it will need color to set it off . . . shake some paprika on it! Remember this, like all sauce hamburgers, is a knifeandforkburger.

THE ELECTRIC BLENDER

Never underestimate the usefulness of the electric blender in the kitchen. You can use it to mix, mash, pulverize—you can even grind your own meat into hamburger.

Get someone to give you one as a present and ask for the kind with many speeds.

The blender makes a gorgeous instant Béarnaise sauce or instand Hollandaise—they are foolproof—and don't forget to use the blender cookbook that comes with a new blender, or better still, *buy* the *Gourmet Blender Cook Book by Paul Mayer.*

THE GOURMETBURGER

This Béarnaise sauce goes especially well with the hamburger. We garnish the finished product with rounds of sliced lemons—dotted with a sprig of parsley—alternating between the top bun quarters around the patty. We call it the Gourmetburger.

BÉARNAISE SAUCE

PART I

3 Tablespoons white wine
1 Tablespoon plus 1 teaspoon tarragon vinegar
1 teaspoon dry tarragon
1 teaspoon shallots, minced
1/4 teaspoon pepper

Place these five ingredients in a small saucepan. Simmer until half liquid and half solid.

PART II

3 egg yolks and 1 1/2 egg whites* (room temperature)
2 Tablespoons lemon juice (room temperature)
1 pinch salt
1 drop Tabasco sauce

1 teaspoon Accent
5 oz. butter, melted
1/4 cup parsley, chopped

Place in warmed blender container egg yolks, egg whites, lemon juice, salt, Tobasco sauce, Accent, and butter. Start in motion for 2 seconds—slowly add parsley.

Now add Béarnaise ingredients (Part I) to Hollandaise (Part II) while still in motion. Result—Béarnaise sauce!

HINT: Keep whirlpool motion in blender by flicking switch off and on again.

*Putting in egg whites is not exactly Kosher, but it gives you a terrific sauce consistency and stretches the recipe. Remember it is a *sauce* and as such should be a bit runny—but not too much! I like it firmed up a bit—let the icebox set it for you.

JACQUESBURGER

This sauce is a most unusual one for the hamburger. It is so good you won't believe it till you've tried it! But—remember it must stand 24 hours before using.

JACQUES SAUCE

2 cups sour cream
a 2" squeeze from the tube of anchovy paste
1 small clove garlic, crushed

Mix well together.

2 Tablespoons red wine vinegar
3 Tablespoons white wine vinegar
1 Tablespoon tarragon white wine vinegar

Mix well together.

1 cup finely chopped parsley
1 teaspoon coarse ground pepper

MIX EVERYTHING TOGETHER – If too thick, add a little *milk* to thin.

6 - 1/3 lb. patties
2 Tablespoons butter
1/2 cup beef stock
2 teaspoons prepared **Dijon** mustard
3 Tablespoons capers
1/4 cup water
3 Tablespoons all-purpose flour
1/2 cup sour cream
salt and pepper

CAPERBURGER

When capers are used in concert with other seasonings, as I have done in this sauce—the end result is overwhelming in beauty.

1. Under-cook the patties in your iron skillet in butter. Remove the patties to a warm spot.

2. Add stock, mustard and capers to the skillet—cover tightly and simmer for 5 minutes. Add water and flour and mix well—cook stirring constantly until thickened. Stir in room temperature sour cream . . . heat through. Serve sauce over patties.

MARGARINE

In most all recipes you can substitute margarine for butter and you'll live longer . . . be richer . . . but is it worth it!?!

CONTINENTALBURGER

Bud Ehresman of Laykin Et Cie created this sauce *with* the hamburger. It won our prize of a crisp five dollar bill. We award $5 to anyone who gets a recipe on our menu!

I said a sauce *with* the hamburger because as you will see from the following recipe it is just that:

In an iron skillet heat 1/2 cube butter and 1 teaspoon olive oil.* Now place in 4 large sized hamburger patties. When juice starts bubbling on top, turn over and add to the pan another 1/2 cube butter. To 1/2 pint of half-and-half cream add 3 tablespoons of Worcestershire sauce and 3 drops of Tabasco sauce. Mix together and pour over the patties. When the patties are cooked to your fancy, place them on a warm platter.

Now with a metal spatula scrape the pan and then pour all from the pan over the patties. Serve with (or without) a hamburger bun or serve with steamed rice—garnish with sprigs of parsley! You will never find a better sauce for hamburger steak, rice and french cut string beans . . .

Nothing could be healthier and sexier than this!

*The olive oil will prevent the butter from spattering!

THE HAMBURGER AU POIVRE (PEPPER STEAK)

It is odd that France which can do, and does do, so much more with food than any other nation has done nothing with the hamburger! Anyway, we have . . . try this one for size.

There is only one pepper to use and that is whole peppercorns ground fresh. Preground pepper is an irritant and the flavor is lost through oxidation. Keep a pepper mill at your elbow for cooking.

Over an uncooked hamburger steak grind some coarse fresh pepper. Gently pat it into the patty. Cook and presto—a steak au poivre . . . To be a realist, as is my wife, flame over 2 oz. of cognac just before serving.

59

THE HAMBURG HAMBURGER

Now here is a hamburger that is really elegant!

Form 4 - 1/3 lb. patties—shake with nutmeg. In an iron skillet add 1/4 of a quarter pound stick of butter—when butter is melted fry the patties.

When you turn the patties, place on top of each one a 1/4" slice of liver sausage. When the patty is done, place it on the bottom toasted roll and on top of the patty put a thin slice of Bermuda onion and 3 long thin slices of dill pickle.

Mop with the top of the roll the juices in the frying pan. Now top the sandwich and eat quick before it gets cold!

CAST IRON SKILLET

I believe every kitchen should have a cast iron skillet to use exclusively to pan fry hamburgers. This pan should never be washed out with water but rather wiped smooth and clean with salt and paper towels.

Next time you are in an oriental tourist store buy a dozen small paper Japanese parasols. They are truly great for eye appeal for a hamburger . . . and for the kids . . . "Eat the hamburger 'darling' and you can have the nice umbrella . . ."

Just stick one through the top of the hamburger and serve!

63

KYOTOBURGER

This sauce is different—it is very country Japanese and darn good! Just put all the ingredients in a pot and simmer for 5 minutes.

KYOTO SAUCE

1 cup mayonnaise
2 teaspoons beef base
1 cup cream
3/4 cup onions (green)—slice lengthwise then cut into 1" strips
3/4 cup white onions cut into 16 small wedges—smaller than the green onions
4 teaspoons sugar
2 teaspoons Accent

4 teaspoons soy sauce
3/4 cup sliced mushrooms
1 teaspoon lemon juice
garlic juice

Now dissolve in water *2 teaspoons of cornstarch* and add and stir and cook till the consistency of gravy. Pour over your hamburger. To garnish stick a miniature Japanese parasol in the patty—don't forget to quarter the toasted top of the bun and place them around the patty mounted bun.

TERIBURGER

This recipe is not cooked—but it should be let set for 24 hours before using. It came from Grace LaBorte, a Korean lady and a dear waitress for 15 years at The Hippo. It is one of our most popular hamburgers. Decorate it with a Japanese onion pick and garnish with o-ro-shi (thin julienne of Japanese radish). Dunk the roll top as well as the meat into the sauce—or pour the teriyaki sauce over the whole thing and eat with a knife and fork.

TERI SAUCE

6 oz. soy sauce
3 oz. water
5 Tablespoons white wine (Chablis)
1 Tablespoon plus 1 teaspoon oil
1/4 cup white sugar
1 1/2 oz. ginger
1 oz. mashed garlic
1/2 teaspoon Accent
6 oz. pineapple juice

66

SWEET & SOUR SAUCE

1/2 cup brown sugar
3 Tablespoons white wine vinegar
1/4 cup tomato sauce
1/3 cup tomato ketchup
1/2 cup pineapple pieces and juice
3 Tablespoons soy sauce
1 cup green bell pepper pieces
1/4 teaspoon minced garlic
1 cup onion heart pieces
6 halved maraschino cherries
2 Tablespoons cherry juice
1/2 bouillon cube
1/8 teaspoon ground ginger
3 Tablespoons cornstarch
6 Tablespoons cold water

THE CANTONESEBURGER

Now here is our own Hippo Chinese Sweet & Sour sauce . . . just like it says, but not too sour. It is glorious on the hamburger—magnificent on a hamburger steak and should be served with Chinese asparagus (Page 110). Garnish with a lichee nut* skewered with a bamboo pick.

This sauce should be made with great care, both in measurement of ingredients and proper procedure. Otherwise, as Confucius say: "It is sin calling to Heaven."

Combine all ingredients on the opposite page—except the cornstarch and water—and bring to a boil. Now combine the cornstarch with the water and add to the sauce . . . stir until thickened.

*The lichee nut served with some of our hamburgers is considered a Chinese luxury. You can buy them canned in a sweet sauce. We buy ours fresh in Chinatown. They come in a crisp textured brown shell. The nut is inside this easy-to-open shell, it is soft dark meat—and is most flavorful. Inside the fruit is a pit which you spit out!

BOMBAYBURGER

This is a delightful curry designed to go with our beautiful Western beef. The more condiments, the better.

For a garnish we add shredded coconut and mandarin orange segments, and a colorful Japanese paper flower. The boys love it and so will you and your ole man! (That is that for the generation gap slang!) If you want to have more fun with this hamburger—add traditional curry condiments . . . like, chopped peanuts—chopped crisp bacon—chopped onion—coriander (Chinese parsley)— Chow Chow pickles—ad infinitum.

Sauté onion in vegetable oil till transparent. Add chopped apple and cook and stir till mushy. Add the remainder of the items . . . stir and simmer for 1/2 hour. Serve over the hamburger.

MAKES 1 QUART:

1 cup chopped onion
1 cup chopped apple
1/4 cup vegetable oil
1 tender squeeze of garlic
1 Tablespoon curry powder
1/4 cup ketchup
1 Tablespoon lemon juice
1 pinch salt
1 can beef consommé
   1/2 can water

71

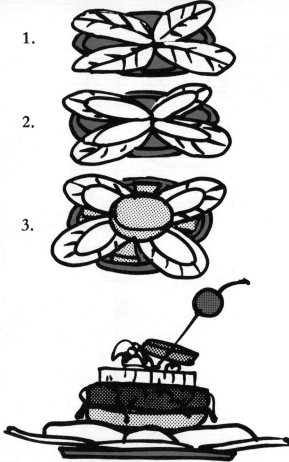

1.

2.

3.

2 lbs. hamburger formed into 6 patties
24 large ti leaves* (or Romaine leaves)
Ingredients for 24 banana fritters (see page 146)
6 hamburger buns
18 oz. Cantonese sauce (Page 68)
6 rounds of sliced pineapple
6 water chestnuts
6 maraschino cherries
6 bamboo skewers
6 sprigs of parsley

THE TAHITIANBURGER
FOR 6

The Tahitianburger was born out of a rum fantasy while imbibing a Suffering Bastard at Trader Vic's. It turned out to be one of our proudest accomplishments and believe me, when you have built it you will know what I mean!

Have banana fritters (Page 146) ready to cook and Cantonese sauce (Page 69) made. Arrange ti leaves in cross shape on plates, as in Diagram No. 1! Now start cooking banana fritters. Put hamburgers on to cook. When fritters are done to a golden brown—remove them from pan and blot. Put one fritter lengthwise on top of each leaf and ends should touch in the center. Toast hamburger buns and quarter bun tops and place between fritters, as in Diagram No. 2! Put bun bottoms on top of the center platform made by the fritters, as in Diagram No. 3! Skewer the water chestnuts and deep fry for 3 minutes. When patties are cooked, place on bun bottoms and cover with approximately 3 oz. of Cantonese sauce. Top with pineapple ring and stab end of skewer into the pineapple ring. Puncture cherry with end of skewer. Garnish with a sprig of parsley at base of skewer.

* ti leaves: You can get these lovely tropical leaves at your favorite exotic florist.

HAMBURGER BARBEQUE AL FRESCO

— 50 PEOPLE

Don't get all up tight just because you are having an al fresco luncheon for 50 guests . . . It will be a lark with the beloved hamburger! Most of the work for this luncheon will turn to fun for Dad with his charcoal broiler—a spatula in one hand—and a beer in the other!

Now listen carefully. In the morning from 19 lbs. of hamburger form 51 patties (6 oz. each—or roughly 3 to a pound). Set them out on a flat platter, cover the first row with wax paper, then add another row of patties—more wax paper, and then a third row. Never higher than three rows or the weight will squash the bottom patties. Now put them in the reefer till ready to cook.

Now shred thin about 4 heads of iceburg lettuce and mound on a round tray. Outline at the base with parsley and serve with regular kitchen tongs so the guests can pick up the shredded lettuce. Slice 55 thick slices (1/4 inch) of tomato and arrange overlapping on a platter. Put your favorite pickle relish in a bowl—in another bowl empty a bottle or two of ketchup. A platter of Kosher dill pickles sliced lengthwise could be a great addition. Arrange these dishes on a serving table . . . not far from the barbecue.

Now Dad will fit perhaps 10 patties on his grill at a time. (As no group of 50 wants to eat at once, he will find the cooking surprisingly easy, particularly if your guests have been nicely oiled.) Sell the rare* patties first—spatula them onto hamburger buns which have already been sliced and toasted—and don't worry, your guests will find the condiment table and the wine . . . This you will have prepoured from the gallon jug of your favorite red wine! Enjoy yourself and your guests will too!

*See page 4 on how to cook hamburger patties!

Fourscore and ten million years ago our forefathers started guzzling. To honor these illustrious ancestors I created The Monkey In.

First I took the rear storeroom of The Hippo, dimmed the lights—lowered the ceiling—and saw-dusted the floor. To further honor our forefathers, I called it, after them, "The Monkey In" and added "For a Beer." This beer joint reeked with atmosphere, potbellied stove—tinkling piano—candles—checkered tablecloths—uncomfortable chairs—and corny songs. We served beer on tap or by the mug or pitcher—peanuts, pretzels, pepperoni, fun by the round barrel—squares were strictly verboten in The Monkey In. On Tuesday and Sunday evenings we served a FREE buffet supper, a true experience—in the culinary and economy art. From this experience we learned to make meat loaf and meat balls—some the size of golf balls, others as large as tennis balls. We mix-ed meat in with a lot of cooked rice to save money! And sometimes we put them in with spaghetti or other pastas or sauces . . . or our own mushroom gravy. At times we made hamburger meat enchiladas. We just wrapped a tortilla around some Mexican spiced hamburger*—put a can of to-mato sauce over the top and studded it with Monterey Jack cheese . . . and put them under the broiler until they bubbled . . . with a cold draft beer it was delicious!

*See page 79.

76

77

MEXICAN HAMBURGER MIX

This Mexican Hamburger Mix is the same formula we use to fill our enchiladas and for our tacos and tostadas. We also use it for the Tacoburger.

MEXICAN BEEF MIXTURE

1 lb. hamburger
1/4 lb. chorizo
1/2 cup chopped onions

1/2 kernel pressed garlic
1 cup canned enchilada sauce (8 oz. can)

Sauté the hamburger for about 18 minutes in an oiled iron skillet—breaking constantly with a fork into small granules. Now add chorizo—a Mexican spiced sausage—it comes in mild, hot, and extra-hot—I prefer to use the hot because it has the best flavor. Add your onions and garlic. Continue to fork and fry until the chorizo is melted. Now drain off the excess liquid that has accumulated in the pan and add the enchilada sauce. I use the Las Palmas canned enchilada sauce—it is pretty hard to beat. Simmer covered for 15 minutes.

This recipe is plenty of meat for: 4 enchiladas—page 80, or 8 tacos—page 81, or 6 tostadas—page 82.

HAMBURGER ENCHILADAS

In an iron skillet heat about 2 inches of vegetable oil. Do not let the oil smoke. Dip each tortilla into the oil for about 20 seconds. Paper blot dry. Brush tortilla with enchilada sauce. Mound some of the Mexican Hamburger Mix (Page 79) down the center of the tortilla—ROLL—place on flap down. Cover with enchilada sauce (Page 79). Sprinkle over with a generous amount of shred—ded Monterey Jack cheese.

Broil till cheese melts. Serve with a glob of sour cream—crown with a black olive. Dress the plate with some shredded lettuce.

TACO WITH MEXICAN HAMBURGER

On page 79 I explain how to make the Mexican Hamburger filling for a Mexican taco. But first buy some crisp tortilla shells—folded in half—warm them in the oven. Put about 2 tablespoons of meat mixture in the crevice of the shell—next put some chopped tomato pieces—add some shredded lettuce . . . spoon on top of this and let drip into the cavity some green chile salsa (you can buy this in a can). Sprinkle with parmesan cheese and garnish with an olive.

In you really want it *snappy*—include a spoonful of guacamole (Page 105). The kids dig the Taco!

THE TOSTADA

Now here is a new one for the hamburger—the Tostada. It is a big seller—looks beautiful—and tastes even better.

Deep fry a tortilla till crisp. Top with 3 oz. of refried beans (or try some of our chili beans, page 3). Cover with 1 slice of cheddar cheese, now add 1 1/2 oz. of Taco meat. Heap on top of all of this a handful of shredded lettuce and form into a mound. Top the mound with 1 spoonful of green chile salsa . . . top that with a glob of guacamole, and that with an olive and parsley. For a garnish, lay 4 tomato slices symmetrically against the sides of the mound—sprinkle with parmesan cheese! Surround the pyramid with wedges of tortilla chips . . . points out . . . I don't think this edifice of the Mexican Americanized sandwich can be beat!

CUCUMBERS IN SOUR CREAM

To a cup of sour cream, room temperature, add 1 tablespoon lemon juice and some coarse ground pepper. Now add a bit of mint chopped fine, and mix with a fork. Peel and rub with a garlic kernel 2 cucumbers and slice them thin. From one bermuda onion slice many *thin* onion rings . . . now mix all together with the sauce in a larger bowl. Serve with a hamburger steak dinner as a succulent condiment.

MEAT LOAF

The early American meat loaf was a dull mixture of ground meat and bread soaked in milk. But, today we jazz up the meat loaf and accent it with our favorite flavors . . . If you are mad for bell peppers . . . add some—same goes for corn— or nutmeg or garlic, etc. . . . or form your meat loaf around a long thin whole carrot.*   It's fun when you carve into the loaf and see the round of carrot embedded in the meat slice and it has a great texture!   Other effective eye appeals and new tastes for the meat loaf are a row of hard boiled eggs— or a center of pre-cooked spinach or whole *uncooked* mushroom heads— or just scatter pimento stuffed green olives or strips of pimento or little nutmeg! Any of these additives will prove delicious and effective when mixed in with the loaf. They all give a beautiful look and tasty effect. By the way, it will take about one hour to cook any meat loaf in a 325° oven—and don't forget as soon as you taste your loaf, rave about it—it will work psychological wonders on your guests' taste buds!

*If you do put a carrot in your meat loaf—remember it must be parboiled to the touch of a tooth-pick.

Some like it hot—some like it cold—but whatever you do, don't eat it after its 3 days old!

MEAT LOAF GARNISH

Garnish up your hot meat loaf! Place the loaf on an oval platter with a ring a'round of baby carrots . . . and small boiled new potatoes—make a ridge of parsley leaves along the top of the loaf— A full bouquet of parsley on one end. *Cold* meat loaf should be served sliced on a bed of shredded head lettuce or . . . Arrange meat loaf on a platter—arrange around the loaf canned Celery Victor or asparagus spears in lettuce cups—crisscross with pimento strips, dab with minced parsley!

With the meat loaf . . . be sure to serve a red wine—California red is remarkably good—buy it by the gallon or 1/2 gallon—it's cheaper that way. If you don't have stemmed wine glasses—use "old fashioned" glasses, that's the way we serve it at The Hippo . . . and it's fun!

ECONOMY 8 LB. MEAT LOAF — FOR 16 PEOPLE

Now here is a great old fashioned meat loaf . . . inexpensive and superb for a cold *buffet* summer supper and your guests won't need knives!

5 lbs. ground hamburger
2 cups chopped onions
4 eggs
2 lbs. stale bread (approximately 1 loaf)
1 teaspoon pepper
1 teaspoon salt
2 cups celery tops—chopped
2 Tablespoons Maggi seasoning

Knead it all together with your nice clean hands. Form two loaves. Bake at 325° F. for one hour.

Don't forget the parsley garnish on the platter—lots of it! Parsley is cheap and high in eye appeal.

86

A TYPICAL BALKAN MEAT LOAF

2 lbs. fresh spinach or two packages (10 oz. each) frozen chopped spinach
1 lb. round steak, ground

3/4 cup finely chopped onions

1/2 teaspoon grated nutmeg

1/4 teaspoon ground cinnamon

1 cup cooked rice

2 eggs, slightly beaten

3 slices of bacon

salt & freshly ground black pepper

1. Preheat oven to 350° F.

2. If fresh spinach is used, rinse it well in several changes of cold water to rid it of sand. Drain, place in a kettle, and cook in only the water that clings to the leaves. Chop well. If you want to save time use frozen spinach. Cook it according to the directions on the package. Be sure to drain.

3. Mix well with your hands—spinach, beef, onions, salt and pepper to taste, nutmeg, cinnamon, rice and eggs. Pack mixture into a buttered loaf pan (9 x 5 inches). Arrange the bacon over the top. Bake for one hour—or until firm. Serve the above with our own beautiful tomato sauce*!

*Page 132

ALA

A wonderful substitute for rice, and it goes great with meat loaf, and casseroles with hamburger.

Buy a box and follow the directions!

COLD MEAT LOAF SANDWICH

Never underestimate a cold meat loaf sandwich . . .

Toast 2 slices of bread, spread one side with Dijon mustard and the other with a *quality* chili sauce. Add a little gourmet relish of pickles and vegetables. If you like—some mayonnaise. What a great Sunday lunch for the family! A real *home* treat—you will *never* find it as good in a restaurant—not even at The Hippo!

Serve your green salad *after* the meat loaf. Serve cheese and crackers with it. If you are having wine—make your salad dressing with fresh *lemon* juice.

BELGIAN MEAT LOAF

If you want a Belgian-type meat loaf, make 1/3 of the meat ground *pork*, add a couple of eggs, chopped cooked vegetables, and cooked macaroni—squash together—bake in the loaf tin.

MEAT LOAF & BALLS
BREAD-BREAD CRUMBS-OATMEAL

Bread used in meat loaf or meatballs should be a day or two old. Work pieces into the meat. DO NOT milk soak the bread—the object is to have the bread soak up the *MEAT JUICES*. If you have an electric mixer make bread crumbs! Another alternative is to use one minute dry oatmeal—very healthy. Use approximately 1 cup oatmeal to 1 pound of hamburger!

MEATBALLS . . . are flavored like meat loaf. You can probably use any meat loaf recipe in this book and just form it into meatballs . . .

When you are forming meatballs keep your hands wet with water as this will keep the meat from sticking to your hands and assist in forming a nice even look.

Fry your meatballs in a skillet—with butter—bacon fat—or their own juices. When the balls are browned pour your sauce* over. Add a little water if necessary and simmer for 1/2 hour. Great with noodles—spaghetti or what pasta have you?!

*Any of our sauces for the hamburger go well with meatballs. Just fry the balls and add your choice of sauce.

CALIFORNIA MEATBALL AND RICE CASSEROLE (8 SERVINGS)

1 cup uncooked regular rice
1 large can (1 lb., 12 oz.) tomatoes (No. 2 1/2 can)
1 Tablespoon butter
1 1/2 teaspoons salt
1/2 teaspoon dried rosemary (or 2 sprigs fresh rosemary)
1/4 teaspoon crumbled dried sage (or 1 sprig fresh sage)
1 pound ground beef
1 1/2 teaspoons salt

1/2 teaspoon pepper
1/4 teaspoon powdered savory
1 egg, slightly beaten
1/2 cup finely dried bread crumbs
1/4 cup milk
2 Tablespoons butter
1/2 cup shredded Cheddar cheese

Mix rice, broken-up tomatoes, butter, salt, rosemary and sage in top of double boiler. Heat to boiling point, stirring occasionally, then cover and cook over boiling water until rice is done—about 25 minutes.

Meanwhile, mix together ground beef, salt, pepper, savory, egg, bread crumbs, and milk. Form into 24 balls about the size of golf balls. Fry in an iron skillet with melted butter until brown on all sides. Turn rice into greased 2-quart casserole, place meatballs on top, and sprinkle with cheese. Bake, uncovered in a 350° F. oven for 20 minutes. Makes 8 servings of 3 meat balls a piece.

STUFFED VEGETABLE

Here is a colorful dish with 4 varieties of vegetables—all stuffed.

Two will be ample for each person. I like a tomato sauce served with this, but then—I am a *sauce* man.

Cut a slice from each pepper and discard the seeds. Cut a slice from each tomato and scoop out the center. Chop the tomato insides and add it to the ground beef. Cut a slice from each squash and eggplant, scoop out the centers (chop the centers) and add to the beef. Sprinkle the vegetables with salt and pepper.

Mix the ground meat and vegetables with the rice, onions, parsley and garlic until thoroughly blended.

Fill scooped-out vegetables, not too tightly, with the mixture and arrange them in rows in a kettle or baking dish. Add water just to cover the bottom of the pan. Cover tightly.

Bake in an oven (325° F.) for about one hour or until the vegetables are tender. You may have to add a little more water to the bottom of the pan.

3 small green peppers
3 firm tomatoes
2 small green squash
2 small long eggplants
1 1/2 lbs. lean beef, ground
1/2 cup uncooked rice
2 medium onions, finely chopped
3 Tablespoons minced parsley
1 minced garlic clove
salt & freshly ground black pepper

SVENSKA KOTTBULLAR (SWEDISH MEATBALLS)

1/5 pint of table cream
3 whole eggs
3 slices dried white bread

2 onions, very finely grated
pepper and salt to taste
5 medium sized mashed potatoes

Stir the above well, then add the following ground meat:

1 lb. beef
1/2 lb. veal
1/2 lb. pork

Now add slowly 1/3 cup of cold water. Thoroughly mix with an electric mixer. Roll mixture into small balls. Let set for approximately 1 hour.

Fry the meatballs in butter till well cooked and brown. Man, they will be just like in the old country—Serve with or without gravy—try cranberry sauce with them!

CASSEROLES

For those of you who work and want a dish that can be prepared in advance—try any of these casseroles.

They may be prepared the night before . . . Just remember to keep them refrigerated between the time of making and oven time. It should take about 3/4 to 1 hour in a 350° F. oven to get good and hot. If it is frozen—it will take twice as long!

PASTA : SPAGHETTI, NOODLES, MACARONI, ETC'

To cook, put pasta in a pot of boiling water that looks much too big for the amount you are cooking—salt it—add 1 teaspoon of olive oil, and keep it at a rolling boil. Cook about 7 minutes. The pasta should not be soft. Put in a colander and under the hot water faucet for 1/2 a minute— now put back in the still hot saucepan and add ample sweet butter and shake on Parmesan cheese . . . or your favorite meat sauce . . . or another sauce you crave.

BEEF & MACARONI CASSEROLE

It is hard to beat this casserole . . . It has protein, vegetables, starch and glorious flavor. Serve with a tossed green salad and hot french bread. This recipe is for 8 servings.

1. Heat the oil in a large heavy skillet. Sauté the onion and garlic in it until tender and golden. Add the celery and beef and cook until the meat loses its red color.

2. Add the mushrooms, stock, tomato paste, tomatoes, salt and pepper. Bring mixture to a boil and simmer for 1 to 1 1/2 hours, stirring occasionally. Add more stock if the mixture becomes too thick.

3. Preheat oven to 350° F.

4. Mix the sauce with the oregano, basil, macaroni and spinach and pour into a buttered three-quart casserole. Top with the crumbs mixed with the cheese. Bake for thirty minutes, or until bubbly hot and lightly browned.

1/4 cup olive oil

1/3 cup finely chopped onion

2 garlic cloves, finely minced

1 1/2 cups diced celery

1 1/2 lbs. beef chuck, ground

1 pound fresh mushrooms, sliced

1/2 cup beef stock or canned beef broth

1 can (6 oz.) tomato paste

2 1/2 cups (1 - 1 lb. 3 oz. can) Italian-style tomatoes

2 teaspoons salt

1/2 teaspoon freshly ground black pepper

1/2 teaspoon dried oregano

1/2 teaspoon dried basil

8 oz. small elbow macaroni, cooked and drained

1 package (10 oz.) frozen spinach, cooked and drained

1/2 cup buttered soft fresh bread crumbs

1/3 cup grated Parmesan cheese

97

PIROSHKI (RUSSIAN FOR "SMALL PIES")

2 cups flour
1/2 cup sour cream
2 Tablespoons butter
1 egg yolk

Mix melted cooled butter with sifted flour; then add sour cream and knead a little. Toss on board, dredge with flour and roll out. Cut into round pieces with a biscuit cutter. Place a spoonful of filling in center of each of the Piroshki and close tight . . . pinching into oblong shape. Brush with egg yolk;* bake in moderate oven until crust is brown.

*This gives a nice brown glazed look.

FILLING FOR PIROSHKI

1/2 lb. chopped hamburger
1 onion, chopped
1 Tablespoon butter
salt & pepper to taste

Brown the chopped meat in butter with onion and seasoning. Hardboiled eggs, cooked cabbage or rice may be used in place of, or with, the meat for excitement.

1 1/2 lb. ground lamb

—the leg is the best but your butcher can give you
  less expensive cuts to grind

3 oz. olive oil
2 eggplants
1/4 lb. pine nuts
2 medium white onions, chopped
1 - 8 oz. can tomato sauce
1 - 6 oz. can tomato paste
2 pinches of cinnamon

GROUND LAMB AND EGGPLANT CASSEROLE ALA JACQUES

This recipe is made with lamb—ground like hamburger—I'm sorry that it can't be made with beef and I have never served it at the Hippo, but it's so good I had to include it anyway.

This is a recipe I put together some time ago. It got the nickname Jacques because when I was a bachelor I took an extended jaunt in France through the wine countries and Paris, and came home with a very *frenchie* moustache and Herb Caen dubbed me "Jacques." Frankly, this dish is anything but French. In fact, it has a sort of Syrian flavor and could well be accompanied by a glob of yogurt and stuffed cold grape leaves.

Cut eggplant in 1 1/2" slices. Do not skin. Oil the baking dish with olive oil. Place eggplant rounds in dish. Brush tops with olive oil and cut in quarters each round. Bake 375° F. for 15 minutes. Saute the onions in an iron skillet with olive oil till they are transparent. Now add ground lamb—braise lightly—separate with a two pronged cooking fork. Add salt and pepper to taste, 2 pinches cinnamon. Add pine nuts and tomato sauce. Continue to fork the ingredients. In a medium size casserole spread a layer of eggplant, dab with tomato paste, cover with the ground meat mix . . . now another layer of eggplant, etc. Cover and bake for 30 minutes at 350 F. Serve hot—or warm—or room temperature. Serves 6.

HAMBURGER PIE

Find a biscuit mix following the directions—roll in a circle to fit a round 9" pie pan.

In your iron skillet sauté in a tablespoon of olive oil 1 1/2 cups finely chopped onions till they turn transparent. Add in 1 lb. hamburger. Fork meat into small pieces for a few minutes—or until all meat loses its red color—salt and pepper and add one tablespoon Worcestershire sauce. Spread the dough in the pie tin and pour in meat mixture. Now beat 2 eggs and mix in 1 cup cottage cheese. Pour over meat. Sprinkle with paprika. Bake for 30 minutes at 375° F.

HAMBURGER AS HORS D'OEUVRES

Buy yourself a Japanese hibachi. Put it in the living room for your cocktail party and build a char-coal fire in it. When it gets good and glowy, it's ready for cooking!

Next to the hibachi have a plate of bite-sized rounds of unadulterated hamburger, some bamboo skewers—let your guests roast their own—they'll love it!

Have near a neatly and nicely arranged group of small plates or bowls containing dip condiments, i.e. ketchup, Chinese mustard*, Dijon mustard, teri sauce (see page 66), toasted sesame seeds (see page 12).... and let your guests cook and dunk and get drunk till their hearts content!

HAMBURGER ROUNDS WITH MUSTARD are another great hors d'oeuvre. Form a small ball of hamburger and poke a dimple on top and *fill* with a variety of prepared mustards—place them on a cookie tin and broil—serve hot. Or you may set the round on a thin round of toast before broil-ing.

*Here is a Chinese Mustard recipe from Olive Wong of The Hippo. Look out—It's hot! Coleman's (dry) mustard and cold water to desired thickness. Mix well. Then stir in a little olive oil with chopsticks. Wow!

STEAK TARTARE

We call it the Cannibalburger.

Grind coarse—scrape—or finely chop the leanest and best steak meat you can afford.

To 2 lbs. of the fresh ground cold meat add a little French Dressing to soften the steak. Mix in—

3 lbs. drained capers
1/4 cup finely chopped onions
4 mashed anchovies

Add salt, coarse ground pepper and
Worcestershire sauce to taste.

Serve in a mound garnished with whole anchovies and sprigs of parsley—surround with small squares of pumpernickel bread or dry toast rounds—or form the meat concoction into small balls and roll in chopped parsley.

If you serve steak tartare as a main course, let your guest mix in his own condiments—but do put a raw egg yolk in a hollow on top of the steak mound.

GUACAMOLE

We serve Guacamole at The Hippo on the hamburger and call it the Olēburger* and we serve Guacamole ala carte with toasted wedges of taco chips . . . It is a South of the Border creation where avocado and garlic and lemon and hot sauces are native and cheap. Here is the recipe:

GUACAMOLE

1 Tablespoon lemon juice
2 avocados
1/8 teaspoon granulated garlic
1/4 teaspoon Tabasco
pinch salt
the whole avacado seed

Blend the first five ingredients together with a fork until the consistency of creamed cottage cheese. Place the avocado seed in the bowl of Guacamole to prevent it from discoloring.

*On our menu it reads: "The hamburger topped with guacamole—surrounded by tortilla chips and tomato—viva el Hippo!"

GAZPACHO

This cold soup . . . Spanish in origin . . . would be ideal to serve to guests before a hamburger dinner. It has a beautiful taste and great texture. But it does require a lot of chop chop chopping. Serve in bowls or for fun in an old fashioned glass and remember an ice cube in each serving! To make life easier—pass it around *before* you seat your guests.

4 large very ripe tomatoes, peeled and chopped
1 large cucumber, peeled and chopped
1 medium sized onion, finely minced
1 green pepper, seeded and finely minced
1 cup tomato juice
1 Tablespoon wine vinegar
3 Tablespoons olive oil
1 small clove garlic, mashed or minced
salt & pepper to taste

Mix the tomatoes, cucumbers, onion, green pepper, tomato juice, vinegar, oil, and garlic; add salt and pepper to taste. Chill soup until icy.

AVOCADO GRAPEFRUIT COCKTAIL

Here is a *cool* "cocktail" for before a hamburger or meat loaf dinner.

For three people use: 1 avocado, a large can grapefruit sections. In a small bowl pour 1/2 the grapefruit juice and 3 heaping tablespoons Best Foods mayonnaise. Stir with a fork till blended. Now stir in 4 tablespoons of Heinz's chili sauce, 1/2 teaspoon Lea & Perrins sauce and some fresh ground pepper. Arrange the grapefruit sections along with spooned out sizes of avocado into three compotes. Pour over the sauce. It will be remarkably delicious and a perfect balance for a hamburger meal.

WOK (SOUNDS LIKE "SOCK")

Never underestimate Chinese style cooking. It is certainly different from Western cooking. To get best results get a heavy, steel WOK. A very important cooking utensil to own. It is a pan wider than deep, and round-all-around. They used to be made of iron and were used over a wood burning stove. It has one or two handles. Today it comes with a metal collar that adjusts nicely over gas or electric burners. Don't buy an iron WOK—they rust and require too much effort to keep up. Get a WOK in natural steel.

The WOK is great to cook vegetables in. The Chinese do a beautiful job on vegetables. Never overcooking them—the WOK is great for cooking brown and crumbly hamburger as in . . .

CHINESE STYLE HAMBURGER HASH

Throw in the greased and pre-heated WOK 1 pound of loose hamburger meat. Cook until meat gets crumbly, then add and swish around 2 chopped onions, 1 cup sliced celery, 1 cup sliced fresh mushrooms. Now add 1 can of cream of mushroom soup, plus 1 can of water. Now stir in 1/2 cup raw rice, 1/4 cup soy sauce—coarse ground pepper to taste. Now put the whole thing into a greased 2 quart casserole. Bake at 350 F. *covered* for 1/2 hour. Remove top . . . and back in oven for 1/2 hour longer. Serve up in a nest of lovely crisp chow mein noodles . . . you have enough for 8 people.

CHINESE STYLE ASPARAGUS

Use 2 lb. fresh green asparagus for 6 persons—slice them in an extreme diagonal**, about 2" long. Cook them in a WOK*—if no WOK, use an iron skillet—like so . . .

In a mixture of half butter and half warm water (enough to cover well the pan bottom) drop in the cut asparagus—a little soy sauce and pepper. Use low flame and slide continually over the fire . . . or if in WOK, stir briskly. Do not cover, do not overcook. What a great vegetable to serve with the Teriburger or the Teri steak. And, remember never overcook your vegetables. Vegetables should be served crisp—underdone—with all the vitamins in!

*See description of the WOK, page 108.

ASPARAGUS DELLA CASA

The famous old Ameilio's Restaurant in San Francisco used to be famous for this dish . . . it fits like a glove when served with meat loaf.

I take a number of spears of fat, white canned asparagus (about 4 per serving) and place them close together in an open casserole—lace generously with thin slices of butter (not margarine) and sprinkle with lots of grated Parmesan cheese. Place under hot broiler for a few minutes until the butter appears to burn—now it is ready to serve. Surprisingly good even if you are a fresh vegetable fiend—as I am. As a matter of fact, this plate is not the same when made with fresh asparagus! You may also cook and serve in individual ramekins.

WOODEN SALAD BOWL

Always oil a new wooden salad bowl inside and outside with *MINERAL oil* . . . other oils will turn the wood rancid. Never wash out your salad bowl . . . Dry wipe it!

WASHING GREENS (GREEN SALAD)

Wash thoroughly the greens for your green salad bowl. Take each leaf off the head. Wash it in cold water—shake off the excess water and blot on a paper towel. There is only one thing worse than gritty spinach . . . and that is gritty lettuce!

TOSSED GREEN SALADS

Nothing is better to start out a meal with than the mixed green salad—Use any greens you can get your hands on . . . throw in a few dandelion leaves and what-have-you . . . but don't use any *oleander* leaves or you're dead.

For variety add grated well-cooked egg white and grated egg yolk—grate separately—sprinkle either (or both) on top of your mixed green salad. Gives a great flavor and grand texture, and beautiful eye appeal. You can also slice or dice the egg—whatever you do with the *hard boiled* egg learn to *cook* it first (page 118).

And don't forget, never underestimate the fresh raw thin mushrooms in the salad . . . be it a bowl or a plate . . . marinate if you like in a French Dressing (after slicing) for an added zest.

Incidentally, some time when you are serving a salad bowl with French Dressing, do what Hazel Pommer does . . . add a glob of your favorite mayonnaise on top of the salad and toss it in with the French Dressing and greens. You get surprising taste results!

114

Equal parts of the following varieties of lettuce:

Chicory
Australian
Romaine
Red lettuce
or what have you . . .

Tear—not cut—greens into approximate 2-3"sizes.

THE BEST DAMN SALAD

I think this is the greatest green salad with Greek cheese ever made! It is super served with a hamburger or a hamburger steak.

Clean and tear Australian lettuce (or chicory—or a mixture) into a bowl. Break up on top some Greek Feta cheese and a few sprigs of coarse chopped *fresh* coriander (sometimes called Chinese parsley). Over this pour your French Dressing (See page 123). Now toss, now eat, now you may die it's so good!

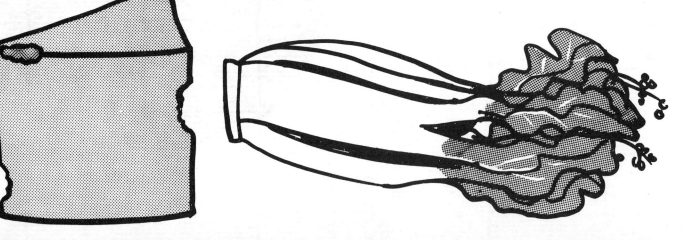

COLD BEAN SALAD . . . AND OTHER SUGGESTIONS

I want to tell you this salad is easy and inexpensive . . . and guaranteed loveable.

1 can kidney beans
1 can garbanzo beans
1/2 can celery—chopped
3 Tablespoons minced parsley
3 long green onions sliced thin—green ends and all

Rinse the beans with water. Drain well and add other ingredients and a sufficient quantity of French Dressing to cling to the salad. Chill and serve for lunch with the good old fashioned American hamburger.

For other variations for this type of a salad, I often add canned mixed vegetables and a small tin of tuna fish, some black olives and anchovies. Sometimes I stuff all of this on a 1/2 of avocado . . . what a lunch for a hot day!

THE EGG AND I

I always keep some eggs at room temperature. I never prepare any dish with a refrigerated egg. I always beat eggs with a French whip!

A SOFT SIMMERED EGG

To cook a hard boiled egg *correctly* is an art and takes time and patience. Hard boiled eggs are hard and tough. Eggs should be soft simmered. They should come out of the water tender and tasteful—not tough like shoe leather. Remember, do not boil your eggs—*coddle** them!

*I quote Webster (with my italics), "coddle [kod'l] **1**. to cook *gently,* as an egg, by heating in water *not* quite at *boiling* temperature. **2**. To treat *tenderly,* as an invalid or a baby; *pamper.*"

SIMMERED EGGS

1. Use sufficient water to more than cover quantity of eggs to be cooked.
2. Place room temperature eggs into water.
3. Slow simmer for 20 minutes.
4. Plunge eggs into ice cold water.
5. To shell these eggs, crack open wide end of egg . . . allow cold running water to enter crack and egg will peel easily.

119

THE HIPPO
THOUSAND ISLAND DRESSING

2 cups mayonnaise*
2/3 cups chili sauce
2 Tablespoons sweet pickle relish
2 Tablespoons green pepper, chopped fine
1 1/3 teaspoons Lea & Perrins Worcestershire sauce
salt & pepper to taste
1/4 teaspoon lemon juice
1 hard boiled egg—cut up into small pieces

First blend the mayonnaise and chili sauce. Then stir in the rest of your ingredients.

*HINT

Make your own mayonnaise—see page 127—you won't believe how great mayonnaise can be . . .
tastes just like you get in France!

HIPPO SOUR CREAM DRESSING

This sour cream dressing is magnificent with thin sliced raw cabbage—whereupon the *cabbage* automatically becomes *cole slaw*. We serve it at The Hippo and garnish with parsley and sprinkle paprika on top.

1 1/4 cups sour cream
3/4 cups mayonnaise
1 pinch salt
1 teaspoon fresh coarse ground pepper
1 teaspoon sugar
2 Tablespoons prepared horseradish

This sour cream dressing is to be the consistency of a sauce. If too thick add a little buttermilk— If too thin, refrigerate!

HIPPO BLEU CHEESE DRESSING

Our customers die for our bleu cheese dressing.

1 cup mayonnaise　　　　　*1 teaspoon Lea & Perrins Worcestershire sauce*
1 cup oil　　　　　　　　　*3 oz. bleu cheese*
1/4 cup vinegar　　　　　　*salt & pepper*

Mix all ingredients together. Now add 3 oz. of crumbled bleu cheese. Let stand for 8 hours.

Here are some herbs to sprinkle on a mixed green salad or mix into the French Dressing to give a variety of flavors:

Basil　　　　　*Mustard*
Coriander　　　*Parsley*
Marjoram　　　*Tarragon*

FRENCH DRESSING

This recipe is for a plain French Dressing . . . very French when served *after* a rich entree.

1/4 cup white wine vinegar
1/4 scant teaspoon salt
1 Tablespoon lemon juice

—Combine ingredients. Stir with a spoon until the salt is dissolved.

Add 1 cup olive oil.

—If you want a thick homogenized dressing, add an ice cube and beat with a fork.

—Stir, pour over enough butter lettuce or limestone (Bib) lettuce for six servings. Toss and serve.

This recipe for **French Dressing** is a little livelier than the previous one:

1/4 cup tarragon French wine vinegar
1/4 scant teaspoon salt
1/4 teaspoon ground pepper
1 teaspoon French Dijon mustard
1 Tablespoon lemon juice

—Stir with a spoon—

Add 1 cup olive oil

—Stir with a spoon—

Pour over your own salad (or see page 112) you have previously made for six servings.

ITALIAN STYLE **French Dressing**

> 1/4 *cup red wine vinegar*
> 1/4 *teaspoon salt*
> 1/4 *teaspoon coarse ground pepper*
> 1/4 *teaspoon Lea & Perrins Worcestershire sauce*

—Stir with a spoon—

Add   *1 cup imported olive oil*
1 clove garlic stabbed with a toothpick left in the dressing overnight

—Stir just before pouring over your salad bowl—

HINTS FOR SALAD DRESSINGS:

1. You can substitute lemon juice for vinegar and *always* substitute the lemon juice if you serve the salad with wine.
2. To say a *vinegar* is a *vinegar* is a Gertrude Steinism. *Imported* white wine and red wine vinegar and white wine vinegar with TARRAGON are a must for your larder.
3. For a variety add different types of herb-flavored wine vinegars—but *never* use cider vinegar!
4. For heaven's sake don't economize on *olive oil*—make sure *it is* imported.
5. For a less rich dressing and better health—use 1/2 olive oil and 1/2 Saffola oil.
6. Always put the oil in last—*Salt will not dissolve in the oil.*

MAYONNAISE (1 1/2 PINTS)

I. ASSEMBLE ALL INGREDIENTS
II. READ THE RECIPE BEFORE BLENDING
III. SET TIMER BEFORE PRESSING SPEED BUTTON

2 eggs
1 pinch of cayenne
1 teaspoon dry mustard

4 Tablespoons strained lemon juice
1 teaspoon salt
1/2 cup olive oil—PLUS 1 1/2 cups to add later

(1) Into container put egg, lemon juice, mustard, salt and 1/2 cup olive oil.

(2) Cover.

(3) Blend 15 seconds on Button 3 (CHOP). Immediately remove inner cap from cover and pour in remaining oil in fast stream. All oil must be added by the end of 15 seconds blending time.

(4) Now blend for 2 seconds on high (LIQUIFY).

(5) Press OFF!

IRANIAN SALAD DRESSING

I want you to know about this salad dressing because it is really something! Make it the *day before* and use it on Romaine lettuce. Of course it will keep fresh for about two weeks. Incidentally, no salt goes in this dressing.

In one quart jar with a tight cover mix:

3 cups peanut oil
1/4 cup burgundy wine
3 Tablespoons red wine vinegar
3 Tablespoons garlic wine vinegar
2 Tablespoons white wine vinegar
1/2 teaspoon DRY mustard
1 1/2 teaspoon celery seed
1 Tablespoon Worcestershire sauce
a dash of fresh ground pepper
1 crushed garlic clove (leave in dressing)

Remember, don't use it the same day you make it!

BASIC BROWN GRAVY

1 1/4 cups water
1/3 teaspoon soy sauce (Kikkoman Shoyu)
1 Tablespoon beef concentrate
1 Tablespoon Lea & Perrins Worcestershire sauce
1/4 teaspoon minced onion
3/4 teaspoon Flavor-Glo
1 pinch salt
1 pinch nutmeg
1 Tablespoon plus 1 teaspoon red wine
4 Tablespoons all-purpose flour blended in 3/4 cup cold water

Place ingredients in a sauce pan. Stir and bring to a boil and down to a simmer. Mix the flour and water and then strain into the gravy—stirring with a French whip until thickened and smooth.

MUSHROOM GRAVY

To the Basic Brown Gravy add 8 oz. of fresh, raw, thin sliced mushrooms—Heat—Pour over a hamburger and you have *your own* Mushroomburger!

MEAT LOAF GRAVY

When your meat loaf is cooked, add 2 teaspoons of flour to 1/2 cup hot water—blend—add to juices in the bottom of meat loaf pan—stir with a fork over fire. Add 1 teaspoon Worcestershire sauce and salt and pepper. If not a rich brown color—add a small amount of Kitchen Bouquet for *the* eye appeal.

NORTH BEACH SPAGHETTI MEAT SAUCE (1 QUART + 1 PINT)

You will never find a better spaghetti sauce recipe than this one . . . takes time . . . but it's worth it and it's *loaded* with meat!

2 Tablespoons olive oil
2 Tablespoons butter
1/2 cup onion, ground
1/2 cup celery
1 1/2 lb. beef

1 cup tomato sauce
3 cups tomato puree
1/4 cup water
1 teaspoon salt
1 pinch garlic

1/4 teaspoon oregano
1 teaspoon San Francisco Seasoning*
2 pinches cinnamon

In your dutch oven over a low flame add the first five items in their order.

Keep forking the meat until it is broken up into beads—no chunks, please! This process will take about 20 minutes. Now the meat should be in good shape and the onion and celery nicely sautéed.

Now add the remainder of your ingredients in *their* order. Now cover the pot and on the lowest heat simmer for 2 hours . . . stirring each 1/2 hour!

*This is a charming mix of dried shallots, Italian parsley, chives, leeks, salt and pepper.

BASIC TOMATO SAUCE

5 large tomatoes
1/3 cup olive oil
1 cup chopped onion
1 cup chopped carrots*
2 garlic cloves—minced
2 leaves sweet basil
1/2 cup butter

(1) Peel tomatoes and cut into eighths.

(2) Heat oil in an iron skillet, cook onions and carrots. Stir until onion is brown. Add the garlic. Stir and add basil and tomatoes. Simmer for 30 minutes. Strain and press mixture through a sieve—return to pot. Add butter and simmer for 20 minutes longer.

For variety add one cup of Sardi's Meat Sauce (Page 134).

*To chop a carrot: Cut carrot in half—face flat half on table . . . cut in thin strips the length of the carrot. Now cut across in about 1/8" pieces . . . Use a French knife for best results.

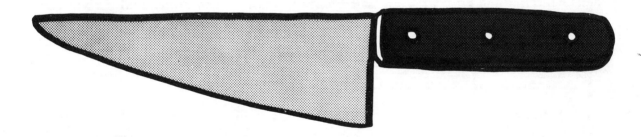

To use a French knife, hold handle in right hand—the heel of your hand pressing down on the end of the blade—now seesaw the knife through the carrots. Result—efficient chop chop without the *chop chop* noise.

SARDI'S MEAT SAUCE (1 CUP + 1 PINT)

(1) Preheat oven to moderate heat (350° F.)

(2) Mix ground beef and ground veal. Spread meat in a baking pan and cook in the moderate oven for 20 minutes. Stir and continue to cook for 10 minutes longer.

(3) In a saucepan combine sage, oregano, salt, pepper, onion, mushrooms, and garlic. Heat, stirring on top of stove.

(4) Spread over meat and continue to cook in oven for 15 minutes longer.

(5) Remove meat mixture from oven and transfer to a larger saucepan.

(6) Add canned tomatoes, tomato puree and tomato paste. Mix well, bring to a boil and simmer for 1 1/4 hours. Correct seasoning with salt, cool, and store in the refrigerator, where it will keep for at least a week, or in freezer. Reheat when needed.

This meat sauce has to be the best . . . it is the sauce used in Sardi's in New York. You can put it on any pastas—you can use it as a base for other sauces—Make a batch of this and keep it in the freezer.

1 lb. ground beef
1/4 lb. ground veal
1/4 teaspoon sage
1/4 teaspoon oregano
1 Tablespoon salt
1/4 teaspoon pepper
1 onion
1/4 lb. mushrooms, ground (4 medium sized)
3 cloves garlic, ground
1 cup tomato puree
1/2 cup tomato paste
4 cups canned tomatoes

135

FRENCH BREAD

One of the beauties of San Francisco is her gorgeous French bread . . . Herb Caen is forever writing of its great sourness and sometimes of its lack of . . . *sourness*. The truth about San Francisco sour dough French bread is that only 3 or 4 French bakeries in town have the real sour dough . . . For some reason the dough survives only in our San Francisco climate—and this dough is like a *mother* and a small bit must be saved from each baking to add to the next batch.

Now sometimes you get a beautiful looking loaf of French bread that is not made with the *real* sour dough. True, the eye appeal may be there—but the sour dough flavor is not!

137

TOASTED GARLIC FRENCH BREAD

Here is a recipe for garlic butter. If you can't get authentic San Francisco sour dough bread, try it on your local *French bread* anyway.

1/2 cup chopped parsley
2 finely chopped garlic cloves
2 cubes of sweet butter

Soften the butter and work it with a fork in a small bowl till it becomes soft and creamy. Work in the garlic—then the parsley—butter it onto the precut* French bread . . . on top—and between each cut then sprinkle with paprika—toast it under the broiler—Watch it! . . . or it will burn!

* To cut a long loaf French bread—cut in half lengthwise through the top center—cut sections to the crust but *NOT* through the crust.

139

MERINGUES

If you have some whites of eggs left over from another recipe, make some meringues. They couldn't be easier to cook and are elegant as a sweet—or molded and filled when cooked. You will need:

3 egg whites
1/4 tsp. cream of tartar
1 cup sugar

3 drops of vanilla
. . . a few grains of salt

Beat your egg whites until frothy. Add cream of tartar and beat until soft peaks form. Beat in sugar slowly. Beat until stiff and glossy. Cover your cookie sheet with waxed paper. Drop small spoons full on the paper—or heap into hollow mounds with back of spoon. You can color these meringues with a few drops of food coloring—just add while beating the eggs.

Put into 400° F. preheated oven. Close door—turn off oven. Leave alone for hours (8 or 10). Never open door—you now have meringue cookies . . . or if you had preferred—hollowed meringue cups that are great when filled with fresh berries and topped with whipped cream!

SOUFFLÉS

I think there is no more elegant a dessert than a soufflé—it is beautiful to look at and regal in flavor and texture. Soufflés used to be difficult for us Americans to make because, first, they were a French creation and second—because we did not have the proper ovens to sustain an even temperature . . . but now we fear not the French culinary art and our ovens today are better than theirs! Remember the soufflé *MUST* rise—that's the fun of the whole thing . . . be sure to use eggs at room temperature and I always whip in an extra WHITE for that important high rise!

A traditional dessert soufflé is chocolate . . . Serve with it whipped cream flavored with a little sugar and a few drops of vanilla—or a bit of rum! Here is a recipe for an easy *CHOCOLAT SOUFFLÉ* and it won't fail . . . if you have *any* egg sense and can read!

CHOCOLAT SOUFFLÉ

Blend together in a saucepan over a low flame:

3 Tablespoons melted butter
3 Tablespoons flour
1/2 cup sugar
1/4 teaspoon salt

Now add and keep stirring:

1 cup boiling milk
2 squares of unsweetened Bakers baking chocolate

When chocolate is melted, remove from fire and add slowly:

4 beaten egg yolks

Let cool.

142

Fold in 5 egg whites, beaten stiff. Pour into the buttered soufflé mold. Bake for 35 minutes at 375° preheated oven.

If the soufflé dish is put into a pan of hot (but not boiling) water, it will have no crust on bottom or sides. Soufflés in the French manner are moist and even slightly *runny* in the center. For a soufflé that is firm all through—bake for 10 to 15 minutes longer.

Serve with a sauce of whipped cream flavored with a little sugar, and a bit of rum!

Don't let the soufflé frighten you . . . I always add one or two extra egg *whites* for that important high rise.

SCANDINAVIAN FRUIT SOUP

The best dessert is fruit—luscious fruit to eat with your fromage.

In Italy everyone eats a fat cylindrical skinned juicy orange. In the State of Washington, U.S.A., they eat their own tart cold apples. Wherever you are, eat the fruit of the locale—if no *fresh* fruit try a Scandinavian Fruit Soup (for dessert) . . . one has to start creating with *dried* fruits when the fresh are scarce . . . those Scandinavians have something here!

Rinse 1 cup prunes (pitted), 1 cup dried apricots, and 1 cup dried peaches. Place in deep pot and cover with 2 quarts boiling water. Let fruit soak overnight. Add the thin yellow rind of 1/4 lemon, grated.

Place pot over medium heat and, keeping the same water, cook fruit until it is quite soft.

Mix 1/2 cup sugar with 2 tablespoons cornstarch. Blend with 1/2 cup dark rum or sherry to make a smooth paste. Stir in a small amount of the fruit mixture, then add the paste to the fruit. Add a pinch of salt. Stir to mix well and turn on heat. Cook for about 10 minutes, or until slightly thickened.

144

Serve hot or cold. I prefer to serve it warm, topped with Swedish cream.

For the fruit topping—Swedish cream:

In a saucepan melt over medium heat 2 tablespoons butter. Add 4 tablespoons flour and stir. Add gradually, stirring constantly, 1 1/2 cups half and half. Continue stirring for about 20 minutes until mixture has boiled and thickened.

Beat until fluffly and lemon-color 2 eggs. Add a little of the hot mixture to eggs and blend well. Then stir eggs slowly into the hot cream mixture. Add 1 tablespoon sugar and 1 teaspoon vanilla. Mix well.

You can also serve this cream chilled in a mold as a separate dessert—it is rich and delicious. This recipe would serve 4.

BANANA FRITTERS AND CINNAMON SAUCE

When I was a lad the *then* old classic San Francisco restaurants served gorgeous banana fritters. They came as dessert topped with real *old fashioned* whipped cream—none of this present day sterilized stuff . . . that *Jack Shelton* so often points out in his *Private Guide To Restaurants.*

Here is my recipe:

BANANA FRITTERS (24)

1 cast iron pot with 3" of vegetable oil
3 cups dry waffle mix, mixed thoroughly with ice water
3 cups ice water
6 ripe but firm bananas, peel and cut each banana in half—now cut in in half lengthwise

Mix water and batter together—the batter must be *cold*—keep it on top of ice. Now dip bananas into cold batter—drip off excess batter.

Now heat oil to 375°. If you don't have a control or a thermometer, drop a drop of batter into the oil (if it goes to the bottom and stays there—it is not hot enough). If it hits the oil and sputters on top it's **TOOO HOT . . . IT SHOULD DROP TO THE BOTTOM AND RISE RATHER QUICKLY TO THE TOP** . . . then your temperature is just right!

Deep fry till golden brown on both sides. You will have to turn them over once. Remove and drain on paper towels.

Top with Cinnamon Sauce—ice cream—or true dairy cream for whipping . . . *if* you can find it!

CINNAMON SAUCE

Here is a recipe for my Cinnamon Sauce. It goes great on our Banana Fritters!

In a small saucepan—mix together the following:

1/2 cup sugar
1 1/2 Tablespoons cornstarch
1/2 teaspoon cinnamon
1/8 teaspoon nutmeg
pinch of salt

Now pour in 1. cup of apple juice—put over fire. Stir and bring to a boil and add 1/4 teaspoon fresh lemon juice. It will cook to a thickness. Then add 2 tablespoons butter. Stir till melted . . . pour over Banana Fritters. Your *lover* will *love it*!

COFFEE

I like coffee. Good old rich strong coffee. It never keeps me awake—I don't think coffee keeps anyone awake. It's all in the head—unless you are not used to coffee and you *over* indulge in it. Buy a Hawaiian Kona roast for a good rich coffee flavor. After dinner I make it 1/2 Kona and 1/2 Expresso. What aroma—what flavor—what a life!

I have never cared much for INSTANT coffees—but I must admit the freeze-dry types make pretty good drinking. Heaven knows they make coffee making a snap, and I do use instant coffee combined with chocolate to make that great mocha flavor for our "Hippo Shakes" a very popular item at the restaurant.

Did you know one pound (that's 80 level tablespoons!) of coffee will make you forty cups?

ECOLOGY

When you handle fresh garlic and onions and many other foods, your hands will take on their odor—and not be pleasant for you or your spouse. To get this smell off your hands hold them under *cold* running water . . . then rub vigorously with 1/2 a lemon. If they still smell, rub with parsley. *DO NOT* ever use hot water—that opens the pores and invites the garlic to stay in.

TIPS

One cup noodles makes 2 cups cooked noodles.

One pound cheese makes about 4 or 5 cups grated cheese.

One cup heavy cream whips to 2 cups.

One pound apples (approx. 3 medium) = 3 cups sliced.

One pound fresh mushrooms = 5 cups raw and sliced.
But 3 oz. dried mushrooms = one pound fresh.

One pound spinach gives 1 1/2 or 2 cups cooked spinach.

A pound of walnuts in shell yields 2 1/2 cups of meat.
And 1/4 of a pound chopped = 1 cup.

1/4 pound of butter yields 1/2 cup melted butter.

One pound of beef cooked = 3 cups minced.
One pound of beef ground = 2 cups.

1/8 teaspoon garlic powder = 1 small clove.

For dried herbs . . . approximately twice as strong as fresh!

151

COOKING EQUIPMENT YOU SHOULD HAVE

Tongs
French whip
Cast iron skillet
Dutch oven
WOK
Soufflé mold
Electric blender

Don't panic over the variety of dry herbs available in markets. Although we often use herbs in our recipes—here are the ones every spice shelf should have:

Rosemary
Laurel leaf (bay leaf)
Parsley*
Spearmint*
Sage*
Garlic
Lemon-thyme
Coriander*

Basil*
Marjoram
Mustard
Tarragon

Please don't substitute powdered garlic—or garlic salt—for the *clove* of garlic—Never-ever!

*Grow your own and use them fresh—they grow easily—try them in your kitchen window box!

IT'S "IN"

In my opinion one of the most amusing things about our customers is what they order . . . With a menu like The Hippo's, and its great variety of the hamburger, a longshoreman gobbles a Cannibalburger, a pregnant lady orders a "Hamburger Sundae"* of course, that's for whom it was put on the menu in the first place . . . Herb Caen comes in and orders a hamburger and tells me how good Bill's is—one time he told me about the marvelous French fries at the Great American Disaster in London where I promptly went to find that they were frozen Irish potatoes . . . so now we serve frozen Idaho potatoes and I must say, in all due respect to my ancestors, they are delicious . . . incidentally the only other frozen item we carry is San Francisco's famous Bud's Ice Cream.

The Hippo has always been a popular place—Mark Spitz came in and didn't order milk . . . Billy Jean King celebrated her birthday here and our whole crew sang "Happy Birthday Ms. Billy" (out of tune, as usual) . . . Dame Margot and Nureyev, the Mayor, the Governor, Rock Groups, High Rollers, the Panthers, Pussicats, and LOL and tourists galore.

Actually, in San Francisco *everyone* eats at **The Hippo**. I suppose that's the interesting and charming part about this Hippo kind of restaurant operation. You may sit next to a Gloria Steinem or a Bobby Riggs or a white-tie opera goer or a "hippie," a worker in soiled overalls or a whole Japanese camera-clicking group . . . any time of the nite—the day—whatever it is—*it's in*—and we love it and we love you . . . all of you!

*A hot hamburger smothered in cold ice cream, hot fudge, topped with a marachino cherry and nuts and served with a Kosher pickle.

SERMON

1969

Because not every businessman and/or restaurateur writes a book—be it ever so humble—I feel a compulsion to include in this relatively primitive cookbook a few words for the youth of today . . . the cooks of tomorrow.

A generation gap or so ago the American businessman posted in his office in large black letters on a white card the immortal word *T H I N K* . . . It later took on the spelling *T H I M K* and understandably! It is too bad that the art of thinking *then* was not applied as our youth apply it today . . . to Peace & Ecology. The future lies in the reach of the youth . . . today he must be an *activist* if he intends to make it . . . AND I know he will—I hope!

INDEX